STEP BY STEP
GROW OYSTER MUSHROOM
SPAWN FOR BEGINNERS

The most effective method to
Grow Oyster Mushroom
Spawn

Eric Brandon

Table of Contents

Chapter one

INTRODUCTION

When you have been developing your own clam mushrooms effectively and getting a charge out of the your rewards for all the hard work, you may get a kick out of the chance to finish the cycle and become autonomous by creating your own shellfish mushroom bring forth.

This instructable depicts how to engender clam mushroom bring forth by means of grain produce move, agar tissue culture move and fluid immunization techniques. These techniques are for the most part low tech (requiring just essential gear), covering the pleurotus ostreatus (winter) and pleurotus pulmonarius (summer) assortments.

Wide Mouthed Jars

Weight Cooker with pressure measure introduced (22 liter – to fit roughly 8 Jars)

Seed or Grain (birdseed or millet appeared to function admirably)

Cotton Wool (to sift through contaminants)

Bowls (to drench grain)

Strainer and Ladle (to wash and channel grain)

Spoon, Knife and Fork (for working with bring forth)

Aluminum Foil (for wrapping container tops and so on in pressure cooker)

Drill (to give air gap in container covers)

For Grain Spawn Transfer:Original Spawn Master (Pleurotus ostreatus (for winter) or

Pleurotus pulmonarius (for summer) purchase on the web and have it conveyed

For Agar Tissue Culture: Scalpel, Alcohol Burner, Petri Dishes, Nutrient Agar and Young Mushrooms

For spore-mass/fluid inoculation:Syringe (5ml), Mushroom Spores, Jar of Sterilized Water

Clean Room:Wood, Plastic, Silicon Sealer, Nails, Staples, Bleach

Chapter two

Prepare Clean Room

To play out the grain vaccinations, you require a sterile domain. Air is loaded with pollutions thus it is essential to lessen the degree of regulations where conceivable. This can be accomplished by building a basic tidy up room. Utilizing flimsy lengths of wood, nail these together to make four divider boards. Spread these boards with plastic sheeting (use staples to connect). Screw the four boards together utilizing sealant along the joins. Run sealant between the base of the dividers and the floor. At last, tape a plastic sheet over the head of the space to frame its roof. For an opening, you can cut an appropriately estimated cut, connecting pipe tape tabs with stick on Velcro going about as clasp. The room ought to have the option to be effectively cleaned down with a detergent arrangement. The room additionally requires a work seat and capacity racks for hatching your containers of bring forth.

Most mushroom tidy up rooms have a HEPA channel introduced to give clean oxygenated air. This instructable uses a low tech approach and will give you elective strategies for limiting air contaminants.

Prepare Jars

Protecting containers are perfect for planning mushroom bring forth. You ought to have the option to discover 1-2 liter containers at your neighborhood jelly outlet (I discovered utilizing 1 liter containers better for fitting into the weight cooker/autoclave). In the event that you can't accepting reasonable containers, at that point reusing old containers is stunningly better (we utilized 1 liter olive containers).

Ensure you clean your containers altogether, all around.

Taking a drill, make a 8mm gap in each container cover. Afterward, this will permit the mushroom generate to breath.

Prepare Grain

Measure out around 2/3 container of grain for every necessary container (the grain will grow marginally as it is drenched). Absorb the grain for 24 hours a bowl of water (utilize enough water to cover the grain totally. In the event that you are utilizing bigger grains, similar to wheat or corn, I discovered stewing the grain for 30 minutes as opposed to dousing assisted with forestalling development of undesirable molds. Wash and channel the grain completely. Liter containers ought to be 3/4 loaded up with grain and covers (with breathing gap) fitted and topped with aluminum foil.

Whenever required (see Step 8 Liquid Inoculation Methods), set up a container of clean water to be disinfected (with a couple of coins added - these assistance to cut up grain bring forth later when shaking the container), fit top and top with aluminum foil.

Chapter three

Sterilization

e the readied grain containers into the changed weight cooker, with an aluminum package of utensils (spoon, blade and fork) to use during the immunization steps. Include roughly 3 liters of water, pouring it cautiously around the containers. Weight cook the containers at 15 psi for an hour. On the off chance that the weight cooker doesn't hold a vacuum, spread the valve with a liquor or fade splashed fabric as it cools. Wash your hands with antibacterial hand-wash and in the tidy up room evacuate containers (while still warm), giving them a shake to permit the grain to stream unreservedly. Permit the containers of sanitized grain to cool totally. Spot the bundle of sterilsed utensils on your work seat for some other time.

Grain Spawn Transfer

There are various techniques to immunize the sanitized grain. One of the most straight forward and effective strategies, is grain bring forth move. You can buy your underlying grain produce on the web and have it conveyed.

Shower down the tidy up room dividers with a 1:20 proportion (5%) of fade to water (It is recommended that a HEPA channel be utilized to clean the air, in any case, this instructable is low tech). Ensure you have showered and are wearing clean garments. Clean your hands with antibacterial cleanser or wear sterile gloves. A face veil and hair top will likewise help lessen tainting (we are extremely messy animals). Open your generate pack (or container) and taking your sterile utensil of inclination, separate the grains prepared to move. Expel the aluminum foil and cover of your container. Move 1-2 desert spoons of the bring forth into your 1 liter container of sterile grain. Rapidly, push a modest quantity of cotton fleece through the cover's breathing gap and connect to the container. At last, shake the container enthusiastically to scatter the grain produce all through the container. Spot on a concealed rack inside the tidy up space to hatch. For pleurotus ostreatus hatch at 24°C (75°F) and for pleurotus pulmonarius (summer) 24°C to 30°C (75°F to 85°F).

Chapter four

Agar Tissue Culture Transfer

Another strategy to immunize your grain, is by first engendering the mushroom tissue on Agar (or cloning). Measure out 5.75 grams of supplement agar powder to 1 cup of clean water (abundant for at least 5 Petri dishes). Start to warmth and mix until the agar is totally broken up. As it bubbles, keep on blending for a moment and afterward expel from the warmth. Empty a meager layer into your Petri dishes and spread with covers. Enclose by aluminum foil and weight cook with your grain (or for in any event 30 minutes at 15 psi). Move your Petri dishes, mushroom tissue and other hardware to the tidy up room. Permit the Petri dishes to cool totally. Splash the tidy up room dividers, seats and floors with 5% blanch arrangement (as before wear clean garments, wash your hands and so forth). A laminar stream seat and hepa channel would diminish pollution during this stage, however it is conceivable (with a higher sullying rate) to prevail without one.

Taking the mushroom by its base, cautiously spit it in two. Spot the mushroom (outside down) on to a perfect surface, ensuring you shield within tissue from contacting anything. Disinfect the surgical tool edge by holding it inside the liquor burner's fire. Lift the top of the Petri dish and cool the surgical tool sharp edge by setting it midway into your agar. With the surgical blade, painstakingly cut a little square from the recently uncovered mushroom tissue. Spot the square of tissue midway into the agar and spread with the Petri dish cover. You may wish to tape the cover (with a clean breathable tape) to decrease the opportunity of sullying. Rehash the procedure, making a point to sanitize the surgical blade before each move. Leave the Petri dishes to hatch.

Brood for pleurotus ostreatus at 24°C (75°F) and for pleurotus pulmonarius (summer) 24°C to 30°C (75°F to 85°F). Colonization should take around 8 to 10 days.

During this time, expel any Petri dishes that has all the earmarks of being defiled with different molds. Once completely colonized (mycelium approaching the edges), the time has come to move the agar to the sanitized grain. Pick just the most solid societies for the immunizations. Sanitize the surgical blade cutting edge, expel the Petri dish top and cut 2 wedges from the focal point of the dish. Expel the aluminum foil and top of the grain container. Utilizing the surgical tool, move the wedges to the clean grain. Rapidly, push a limited quantity of cotton fleece through the cover's breathing gap and append to the container. At last, shake the container enthusiastically to scatter the mycelium from the agar all through the grain. Spot on a concealed rack inside the tidy up space to hatch (temperatures as above). Rehash for each container of disinfected grain.

Cloning consistently (without presenting new strains) may prompt imitate blurring, with resulting societies in the long run losing essentialness and in this way creating less mushrooms. Rather than cloning, spores when sprouted

Liquid Inoculation Methods

One basic method of making your bought mushroom generate go further, is to add it to sanitized water, making a fluid inoculant. Taking the disinfected container of water evacuate the aluminum foil, open the cover and include various desert spoonfuls of grain bring forth (the more produce you use, the quicker your fluid vaccinations will colonize and the less possibility there is for pollution). Join the container's cover and reattach the aluminum foil and shake energetically. Adding a few coins to your water container, before its cleansing, assists with cutting up the grain produce as you shake. Take the needle (5ml) and penetrating the container's aluminum (through the cover's gap), draw 5ml of the fluid inoculant. Take the disinfected grain container, with cotton fleece stopping its breathing opening and infuse the inoculant past the cotton and into your grain. Shake the grain, blending the inoculant all through the container. Spot on a concealed rack inside the tidy up space to brood. For pleurotus ostreatus at 24°C (75°F) and for pleurotus pulmonarius (summer) 24°C to 30°C (75°F to 85°F). You can store the fluid inoculant in the cooler until required.

Another strategy for making fluid inoculant, is blending disinfected water in with mushroom spores.

The stunt with this strategy is to catch the spores. Pick a youthful mushroom, you

Printed by Amazon Italia Logistica S.r.l.
Torrazza Piemonte (TO), Italy